THE ARCHITECTURE AND INFRASTRUCTURE OF BRITAIN'S RAILWAYS

Scotland and Northern England

Patrick Bennett

First published 2018

Amberley Publishing
The Hill, Stroud
Gloucestershire, GL5 4EP

www.amberley-books.com

Copyright © Patrick Bennett, 2018

The right of Patrick Bennett to be identified as
the Author of this work has been asserted in
accordance with the Copyrights, Designs and
Patents Act 1988.

ISBN 978 1 4456 8139 9 (print)
ISBN 978 1 4456 8140 5 (ebook)

British Library Cataloguing in Publication Data.
A catalogue record for this book is available from
the British Library.

Origination by Amberley Publishing.
Printed in the UK.

Contents

Introduction

It is doubtful whether any other functional structure shows as much variation in size, style and ornamentation as the railway station does. This is partly due to the long period during which stations were constructed: from the earliest structures of the 1830s, right through to the present day. Not unnaturally, stations, like other buildings, reflected the prevailing architectural fashion of the day. These styles include the simple elegance of the early Victorian period, the Gothic revival of the later Victorian period, the Arts and Crafts Movement, art-deco and streamline moderne, and post-war concrete brutalism. There was also a reversion to older styles, such as Tudor and Jacobean. As well as style, there was variation in method of construction, reflecting the availability of local materials, and of course size, from the humblest wayside halt to the massive city terminus. Notable in this volume are the stylistic differences between Scotland and England, which are quite pronounced. Certain features, characteristic of Scottish architecture, are found almost nowhere in England.

Railways were not just about passengers, and in fact for most of their existence the transport of freight for most railway companies was far more important in terms of revenue than was the carriage of passengers. Nowadays the transport of goods is much diminished but happily many structures survived beyond their usefulness and were able to be photographed. These facilities include goods sheds and warehouses, cranes, loading gauges, and weighbridges.

Other areas covered in this book include signal boxes and signals, signs and notices of all descriptions, bridges, viaducts and tunnels, and all the equipment and paraphernalia for the servicing of locomotives and rolling stock.

As a railway photographer I had always taken photographs of trains, but I was also interested in everything else that constituted the railway, and increasingly my lens was turned towards those 'non-moving' aspects. What became apparent was that much of this infrastructure was in the process of disappearing. This was partly due to changing technology – the replacement of traditional signalling by a small number of signalling centres – and partly due to the selling off of redundant buildings for redevelopment, often leading to their demolition. The hand of 'modernisation', too, sometimes led to the destruction of traditional railway features. As such, my photography became more and more a way of recording what was soon to be lost forever.

Patrick Bennet
Millay, France
February 2018

Stations

Scotland

Hassendean station is on the Waverley line, which was built between 1849 and 1862. Recommended for closure in the Beeching Report, the station lost its goods services in 1964, became an unstaffed halt in 1967, and closed with the rest of the line in 1969. The railway here was on an embankment and this building is actually of two storeys. It is built of snecked rubble with contrasting sandstone quoins. The waiting room frontage has had a major alteration. The station also had a wooden footbridge, which was something of a rarity. The buildings have since been turned into residential accommodation.

The somewhat rudimentary facilities at Hassendean.

Haymarket is remarkable in being an important railway building, described as 'probably the most important early station building in the country', and also, somewhat incredibly, for nearly being demolished in the 1970s to make way for an office block. Built in 1842 for the Edinburgh & Glasgow Railway to a design by John Miller, it is Georgian classical in style, with a portico supported by four Doric columns.

Stirling station was rebuilt in 1912 in a neo-Jacobean style for the Caledonian Railway by James Miller. Ashlar-built with crow-stepped projecting gables and crenelated wall heads, it is an outstanding example of Scottish railway architecture. Notice the lion-rampant emblem of the Caledonian Railway, both carved in stone and on a plaque on the cast-iron porch. It is listed Category B.

Inside is this wonderful circular booking office beneath a cast-iron and glazed roof.

Another listed building, and another designed by James Miller, Gleneagles, originally called Crieff Junction, was rebuilt in 1919 for the Caledonian Railway. Of particular note are the two towers supporting the cast-iron lattice footbridge, unusual in themselves, and with unusual bay windows.

This L-shaped building at Errol was constructed in 1847, probably by William Heiton, for the Dundee, Perth & Aberdeen Junction Railway. It is built of snecked rubble and has two canopies supported on cast-iron columns and a bay window projecting onto the platform. The chimneys are of brick. The paling fences and cast-iron and lattice footbridge are also listed. Since this photograph was taken the flooring of the bridge has been removed.

The former Aberdeen Railway line was closed south of Kinnaber Junction in 1967. Stonehaven is the only surviving original station on the Aberdeen Railway's main line. Built about 1850, it is a two-storey red sandstone ashlar building in an Italianate style with a glass and steel canopy on the frontage. It is listed Category B.

Kennethmont is situated just past the summit of the Great North of Scotland line from Aberdeen to Keith. The line was opened in 1858. The Beeching Report proposed closure of all intermediate stations between Aberdeen and Inverness, but in fact several stations remained open. However, Kennethmont was not one of them and the station closed in 1968. This photograph, taken in 1992, shows the buildings still in good condition after twenty-four years of closure: a nice, symmetrical, weather-boarded building in cream with plinth, doors, and window surrounds in brown, and a frieze-board in green. The tiled roof is surmounted by two finials and stone chimney stacks.

Just south of Kennethmont is Insch. Looking rather unloved, this rather pretty station building has render over rubble blocks and ashlar door and window surrounds. It came close to demolition in 1992, the date when this picture was taken. A local campaign saved the station, which from 1997 has housed a museum of local history. The buildings were listed Category C in 1999.

Also listed is the waiting room on the opposite platform; this is another weather-boarded building with a brown plinth but with dark grey doors and windows. Of interest here are the frosted and coloured geometrically patterned upper window lights, which are very suggestive of art deco.

Nairn, together with its signal boxes, provides an excellent representation of a late nineteenth-century Highland Railway station. The main building is constructed of coursed rubble with ashlar dressings. The two crow-stepped gables are surmounted by different stone-carved finials. The monogram 'HR' and date of rebuilding '1885' are carved into the left-hand gable, sitting beneath an elaborate dripstone. There are both square and round chimney stacks. It is listed Category B.

On the Up platform are timber lapped-boarded waiting rooms with a sprocketed roof – a feature typical of Scottish station architecture but non-existent in England. The chimney stacks are of stone.

Pitlochry, another Highland station, has many similarities to Nairn. It is constructed of stugged and snecked blocks with ashlar facings. The gables have triangular crow steps and the bay has dripstone mouldings. One of the gables has a thistle finial, the other a crescent moon. The station was rebuilt about 1890. The lapped-boarded building on the opposite platform is very similar to the one at Nairn, except that the chimney stacks are of brick. The picture is completed by the Highland Railway signal box, goods shed and lattice girder and cast-iron footbridge.

The Perth & Dunkeld Railway obtained its Act of Parliament on 10 July 1854 for a line between Stanley Junction and Birnam. Dunkeld (originally Birnam) station was opened on 7 April 1856 and was a terminus until the line was extended to Pitlochry seven years later. Designed by Andrew Heiton Junior, Dunkeld is an outstanding example of Scottish railway architecture. It is built of snecked whinstone rubble with sandstone quoins, and door and window dressings. Points to notice are the decorative bargeboards, the square and octagonal chimney stacks and the two different arches in the entrance porch. For the above reasons the station is listed Category A.

The Maybole & Girvan Railway opened in 1860 and was absorbed by the Glasgow & South Western in 1865. The line was listed for closure in the Beeching plan but somehow survived. Maybole station is built of snecked sandstone rubble with ashlar quoins and dressings. The main building is now a shop, while the building on the right remains in railway use.

Although the line survived, all the intermediate stations of the Maybole & Girvan were closed, including Kilkerran. The two stations are just 4 miles apart, yet built in completely different styles and in different stone. Note the crow-stepped gables and the two chimney stacks with brick replacing the original stone.

The original Girvan station was destroyed by fire in 1946. This replacement in streamline moderne style was built to a design by the LMS architects' department. The rebuilding was not completed until 1951. It is essentially a single-storey brick building with decorative tiling on the upper courses. It is listed Category B.

Located a mile away from the few houses that constitute the settlement, it is not surprising that Barrhill was scheduled for closure under Beeching. The station is an unpretentious single-storey building in snecked rubble, with sandstone lintels and sills. An unusual feature are the brick quoins round the doors. The signal cabin, which houses only the lever frame, was originally at Portpatrick.

Annan has been described as the best surviving early station in south-west Scotland. It was built in 1848 for the Glasgow, Dumfries & Carlisle Railway to the design of William Fairburn. Built of red sandstone ashlar in an Italianate style, it has a magnificent late Victorian glass and cast-iron canopy on the Down platform.

The North West

Liverpool Exchange station was built as a joint station for the Lancashire & Yorkshire Railway and the East Lancashire Railway. Unable to agree on a name, to the ELR it was Liverpool Tithebarn Street, while to the L&Y it was Liverpool Exchange. The argument was settled in 1859 when the L&Y absorbed the ELR. The present building was constructed in 1888, having been designed by Henry Shelmerdine in a free Renaissance style. Notice the columns separating the windows, the cast-iron porte cochère, and the matching projecting clock.

The Garston & Liverpool Railway opened its 4-mile line in June 1864. There were three intermediate stations, to which a fourth, Cressington and Grassendale, was added in 1873 to serve a private estate. Doubtless its proximity to the estate led to it being such a splendid edifice. Listed for closure by Beeching, the station lingered on until 1972. It was reopened in 1978 as plain Cressington.

The Garston & Liverpool became part of the Cheshire Lines Committee route from Liverpool to Manchester, completed in 1873. One of the intermediate stations is Sankey, little altered from the time of its construction: a brick-built, single-storey building with a two-storey cross gable at one end and a single-storey cross gable at the other. Joining the two gables is a canopy supported on cast iron columns. Of particular note are the elaborate bargeboards, each one different.

Earlestown station was built by the Warrington & Newton Railway at the site of its junction with the Liverpool & Manchester Railway. Originally named Newton Junction, it became Earlestown in 1837. It is one of only two triangular stations in Britain. The building is Tudor in style, constructed of coursed rubble and with deep mullioned windows. Also of note are the three sets of different octagonal chimneys. The slate roofed canopy is supported on carved wooden columns. On 23 October 1989 a pair of Class 20s pass through the station with an engineering train. Listed for closure in the Beeching Report, it survived, and is the oldest station building in the world still in passenger service.

Wigan Wallgate, another design by Henry Shelmerdine. This building, constructed in 1896, replaced an earlier one. It is built of brick with red sandstone dressings. Its most notable feature is the large cast-iron and glass porte cochère. It is listed Grade II.

At the time of the electrification of the Crewe–Manchester line a number of stations, including here at East Didsbury, were rebuilt to the designs of William Headley in an ultra-modern style. This is a view taken from the Up platform on 6 May 1989. Unfortunately, all the buildings on this platform have now been demolished.

Poynton is a solid late Victorian building, which is on East Cheshire Council's list of heritage buildings. At the time this photograph was taken in 1989 the staff were clearly taking great pride in the appearance of their station. Note the enamel signs and the luggage trolley with the milk churns. These embellishments were subsequently removed.

Formby station was opened by the Liverpool, Crosby & Southport Railway in 1848, and it became part of the L&Y in 1855. Built in a pleasant style of Accrington brick, the main interest here is the very unusual mosaic showing the station name together with 'L&Y'.

This is the second station built to serve Birkdale. It was opened in 1851 and was originally named Birkdale Park. Of note are the ridge and furrow glazed canopies on cast-iron columns. In the background is the L&Y signal box, a listed structure. However, the line is now controlled from the Merseyrail CC at Sandhills and the signal box is redundant. The Liverpool–Southport line was slated for closure in the Beeching Report, but happily survived.

Ormskirk is something of an oddity. To the west of the running lines is the original station, built *c.* 1848 for the Liverpool, Ormskirk & Preston Railway. Constructed of coursed sandstone rubble with a slate roof, it is now a workshop. To the east is the *c.* 1870 station of the L&Y. This is a red brick building in an Italianate style and has a platform canopy supported on cast-iron columns. Both stations are listed. The further oddity about Ormskirk is that it is at the end of an electrified route from Liverpool. Passengers wishing to proceed further towards Preston have to change here. There is no physical connection between the two lines.

Burscough Bridge station was built *c.* 1855–60 for the Southport & Manchester Railway Company. It is constructed of snecked sandstone in an Elizabethan style, with Tudor arched doorways and mullioned and transomed windows, some of which have hood moulds. It is listed Grade II.

The next station east is Hoscar. The stationmaster's house continues the Tudor theme. The windows have been altered but those on the ground floor have dripstones and the front door has a Tudor arch, while a bay window looks out on to the lines.

Nelson station was opened in 1849 by the East Lancashire Railway. At the time there was no settlement named Nelson, the station being named after an adjacent pub. Only one platform is in use. The main feature of Nelson is the magnificent cast-iron and glass canopy on the island platform.

Originally opened by the Midland Railway in 1876 as Horton, it became Horton in Ribblesdale under the LMS. Listed for closure in the Beeching Report, it succumbed in 1970 but was reopened in 1986. It is typical of a number of stations on the Settle–Carlisle line, having two gabled pavilions linked by a central section that enclosed a waiting area. Since this photograph was taken in 1989 the station has been transformed under the stewardship of the Settle & Carlisle Trust. Changes included the replacement of the clock and also the substitution of decorated bargeboards for the plain ones seen in the photograph.

The Lancaster & Carlisle completed its line from Low Gill to Ingleton in 1861. Apart from Kirby Lonsdale, seen here, there were just three other intermediate stations. The line lost its passenger service in 1954 and freight traffic ceased in 1964. This grand station, built of coursed rubble with ashlar margins, seems somewhat excessive for such a small community. Since the time of this photograph, the buildings have been sympathetically extended.

The other company active hereabouts was the North Western Railway, often called the 'Little North Western' to distinguish it from the LNWR. Their line between Clapham, Lancaster and Morecambe was completed in 1850. Between Wennington and Morecambe, the line closed in 1966. Halton station is an interesting building in that it appears as a rather small adjunct to a massive goods shed. The goods shed is built from brick but the station walls, such as they are, consist of courses of small squared rubble blocks. The front of the station building is a mixture of clapboard and batten-boarding. It is the only station building on the line that survives.

This is Morecambe when it was still functioning as a station. It was built for the Midland Railway in 1907 to a design by Thomas Wheatley. It is built of coursed sandstone rubble with ashlar margins. Below the eaves there are Lombard friezes and there is a continuous drip moulding rising over doors and windows. Of particular note is the large porte cochère with nicely scalloped valancing. Note the bulbous feet of the cast-iron columns, which are presumably there to stop vehicles crashing into them and bringing down the roof. This photograph was taken in 1990; four years later a new Morecambe station opened on a different site and this building passed into commercial use.

These are the 1880s buildings at Carnforth, built to the design of William Tite for the Lancaster & Carlisle Railway. Boarded-up windows hardly make for an attractive appearance but this is a nice Tudor-style building, which was often the fashion for railway buildings in the nineteenth century. Constructed of snecked rubble, points to note are the mullioned and transomed windows and the dripstones above the windows in the gables. The Tudor arch above the door seems to have partially collapsed!

Film buffs among you may recognise the clock and the ramp up which Celia Johnson walked in the film *Brief Encounter*, much of which was filmed at Carnforth. Note also the beautiful railings on the right.

Ulverston station was rebuilt in 1873 for the Furness Railway. It is an Italianate building in coursed red sandstone. Two features of particular note are the cast-iron and glass canopies on both platforms, and the clock tower, which has a pierced parapet and an urn at each corner.

Drigg is a nice ensemble of station building, goods shed and signal box. For their minor stations the Furness Railway had a more or less standard design, although the materials used varied; in this case, random rubble with ashlar margins and string courses. The line was actually opened by the Whitehaven & Furness Junction Railway, which became part of the FR in 1865. Drigg is a request stop on the Cumbrian Coast line.

The station at Askam was opened by the Barrow, Kirby & Dalton Railway. The station was rebuilt by the Furness Railway in 1877. The architects were Paley & Austin. Points to note are the graduated tiles on the gable and the catslide roof over the main buildings, which has been extended to form a canopy.

The North East

The present York station was opened in 1877 to the designs of Thomas Prosser, in collaboration with the engineer Thomas Harrison. It replaced the station of 1841, which had proved inadequate for the mounting traffic levels.

This view of York station presents a confusing picture, for which some clarification is needed. **A** is part of the porte cochère. **B** is the station buildings. **C** is the 1906 wooden tearoom. **D** is the entrance canopy, built *c.* 1906 by William Bell. **E** is the only surviving end-screen to the original design. The others were modified in the BR era. **F** is the octagon vestibule leading to **H**, the (former) Royal Station Hotel. **G** is the main span of the train shed, seen in the previous image.

Beverley was one of the many stations designed for the York & North Midland Railway by G. T. Andrews. It opened in 1846. The station consists essentially of two stout walls supporting an overall slated roof, with the various offices to one side. At both ends are glazed screens. A standard NER 1891 pattern footbridge completes the picture. Since this photograph was taken in 1989 the bricked-in bases to the footbridge have been removed and the roof modified. It has been listed Grade II since 1985.

This tiled map of the NER system appears at a number of ex-NER stations, as well as here at Beverley.

Hutton Cranswick is another work of G. T. Andrews from the same period: a pleasing composition of station house, offices and waiting room, in brick with sandstone plinth (partly obscured by the raising of the platform), string courses and door surround. Perhaps unsurprisingly, the BR(NE) clock has disappeared since this photograph was taken.

Bridlington is an excellent example of Edwardian railway architecture, the station having been rebuilt in 1912 by William Bell. The frontage presents three gables. The central one of these has stone and brick pilasters, while the central two lead to an open-bed segmental pediment containing the date '1912' with a clock below. Two thirds of the frontage is spanned by a glazed canopy supported on cast-iron columns. The right-hand gable contains the refreshment rooms, which were added in 1922. Notice the sign in British Railways North Eastern Region tangerine.

The magnificent glass and cast-iron canopy over Platforms 5 and 6 at Bridlington. Platforms 7 and 8, on the right, are no longer in use.

Hunmanby is on the Bridlington to Scarborough line, where the buildings are also the work of G. T. Andrews. It is a simple and unpretentious building, relieved by panelled walls and recessed windows.

Seamer became a junction in 1846, when the line from Filey was completed. Here we have the typical layout of a country station; on the left is the loading dock, and beyond that is the goods shed. Nearer, on the left, is the 1911 signal box, and behind that the earlier signal box, while the station buildings are on the right. Since this photograph was taken the old signal box, canopy and waiting room on the platform have been demolished.

Thornton Dale has retained much of its character, despite having being closed as a passenger station since 1950. It was opened in 1882 along with the other stations on the Forge Valley line, which ran from Seamer to Pickering. Points to note are the matching gables with their stone window dressings and the glass and cast-iron canopy that connects them.

Weaverthorpe was opened in 1845. It was originally named Sherburn, was renamed Wykeham in 1872 and received its present name in 1882. The eponymous village is 5 miles away! Along with all other stations between York and Scarborough, apart from Malton, Weaverthorpe was closed in 1930. This was to make way for the enormous excursion traffic to Scarborough. Stopping trains would have proved an impediment to these through trains. A plain Flemish bond-built brick station is enlivened by sandstone plinths, a string course, and a pilastered door. Note also the recessed and gauged brick arched windows and door on the ground floor.

A peaceful, timeless scene. This is Heslerton, which, like Weaverthorpe, closed in 1930. Points for modellers to note: the NER type S1 signal box, gable end facing the railway; the gate-wheel-controlled gates supported by posts made from old rails; the signal post supported by guy wires, one of which can be seen just to the right of the signal box; and the post box, half obscured, just to the right of the crossing. No more will the signalman sun himself, as the box is now closed.

Hessay is a station with a chequered history. The East & West Junction Railway opened in 1848 between York and Knaresborough but Hessay was not one of the original stations. However, a single-storey crossing keeper's cottage was provided. This was later given an upper floor and additional buildings were added along the platform when Hessay became a station *c*. 1849. First closure occurred in 1915, followed by reopening *c*. 1922. Final closure to passengers was in 1958 and to freight in 1964. The line was listed for closure in the Beeching plan but was reprieved by Barbara Castle. The station house is now a private dwelling but the station office remains in use for the crossing keeper. Note the lever frame on the platform.

Designed by James Pigott Pritchett, Huddersfield station was completed in 1847 and was managed jointly by the L&Y and the LNWR. The Corinthian portico, flanking colonnades and terminal pavilions give it, according to Betjeman, 'the most splendid station façade in England'. According to Biddle and Nock, it is 'the foremost classical station frontage of its type'. It is listed Grade I.

Wakefield Kirkgate was rebuilt jointly by the L&Y and the GNR in 1857. An ashlar-built classical building with a tall pedimented centrepiece containing a clock, and short wings with alternating pointed and curved window hoods ending in small pavilions, it is listed Grade II.

Penistone station came into existence with the opening of the Woodhead line in 1845, and it became a junction with the opening of the Huddersfield & Sheffield Junction Railway in 1850. The main buildings were on the Woodhead side. In this May 1980 view the gantries and overhead lines of the Woodhead route are visible.

In this second view, taken in the other direction in 1989, the overhead equipment has gone but the station remains much as before. For passengers there is just the rather pleasant canopy on cast-iron columns to give shelter. Note also the running-in board in BR(ER) dark blue. Since this photograph was taken new shelters have been built on both platforms and the buildings behind the canopy have been demolished, but the canopy itself survives.

A building that has not survived is Barnsley station, seen here in 1991. It is an interesting mix of styles. The frontage, with its curved and pointed arches in contrasting brickwork, is Italianate in style, while the roof is more suggestive of France. Points to note are the corbelling on the central pavilion, the dentilling on the wings and the rather nice cast-iron parapet. The station was demolished to make way for the new Barnsley Interchange.

Halifax was designed in a Palladian style by Thomas Butterworth. Completed in 1855, it was altered in 1885 when an additional platform was added on to what had been the frontage. This no doubt accounts for the damage and irregularities evident in this photograph. Nevertheless, it remains a fine example of a late classical building. Points to note are the pedimental centrepiece and the elaborately dentilled cornice.

Hebden Bridge is a remarkable survivor, little altered since it was rebuilt in 1909. As well as the station buildings, the glazed canopies on cast-iron columns and the old signs are all listed Grade II.

Above and below: Shipley is not a listed station, which is unfortunate because the lovely cast-iron and glass canopies seen here in 1989 have all been demolished. Shipley is now a very modern-looking station, with all lines having been electrified. It is one of only two triangular stations in Britain, the other being Earlestown.

The present Skipton station was built for the Midland Railway in 1876 to the designs of Charles Trubshaw. Of note in this view are the two water columns (one of them a 'parachute' type), the wooden signal posts (one with a finial), and the ridge and furrow glass awnings. The line to Skipton was electrified in 1994, leading to the removal of the signals. Skipton was listed Grade II in 1991.

Leyburn is a station on the Wensleydale line, and was first opened under the auspices of the Bedale & Leyburn Railway in 1855. Passenger services ceased in 1954 but the line was kept open by freight traffic. The station house is privately occupied but the single-storey buildings on the right are used by the Wensleydale Railway. It is an unpretentious structure of squared and coursed rubble, and, thankfully, the hideous porch in front of the door has now been removed.

Brompton is another unpretentious disused station. It is built of brick in Flemish bond with sandstone quoins. The line between Northallerton and Stockton was opened by the Leeds Northern Railway. Brompton, along with the other stations on the line, apart from Yarm, Eaglescliffe and Stockton, fell victim to the Beeching cuts and closed in 1965.

Egton Bridge, along with the rest of the stations on the Midlesbrough to Whitby line, was also listed for closure under the Beeching plan, but happily survived. The station building is most interesting; it is constructed in an unusual style of coursed rubble, with two courses of narrow blocks followed by a course of thick blocks. The bay window and chimney stacks are in ashlar. Another unusual feature (for England) are the crow-stepped gables.

This is not the original Stockton station, but is rather the one designed by William Bell in 1893, and is a symmetrical building in red brick with ashlar embellishments. The five-bay building in the forefront is in fact a porch. It has lost the glazing from the roof lights and also its clock. The station buildings have now been converted into apartments. It is listed Grade II.

It would be difficult to recognise the Hartlepool station of today from this photograph. The footbridge and roof have gone and only the near platform remains in use. Happily, the cast-iron columns, with their decorated capitals and elaborate spandrels, have been retained to support the new roof. The panelled wall, seen on the right, which once supported the roof beams, remains.

The Bishop Auckland & Weardale Railway opened its line in 1842 and was extended to Frosterley in 1847, in which year, Wolsingham station, seen here, was opened. The line closed to passenger traffic in 1953 and to freight in 1992. The Weardale Railway has provided sporadic tourist train services since 2004. The station is built of yellow brick with ashlar dressings. The roof consists of stone flags with stone gable copings, surmounted by ball finials. The left-hand gable of the two has an oriel window. The station is listed Grade II.

Sedgefield lost its passenger service in 1952, but the line remains open for freight. A somewhat minimal station, there was just this building at street level and two small buildings on either platform. This was the booking office; the waiting rooms were on the platforms.

Hexham station has listed status for a number of its features, including the platform canopies designed by Thomas Prosser *c.* 1870–71. They consist of cast-iron columns supporting open cast-iron panels, which in turn support kingposts holding up the canopy. From the same period is the wrought-iron footbridge, an early survivor with ring braces in the spandrels. It is also listed Grade II.

Saltburn station was built for the Stockton & Darlington Railway in 1861, probably to a design by Thomas Prosser. The main station feature is this elegant Italianate portico, built in buff brick and dark freestone. The plinth and column footings are in a paler shade of stone. The dark stone and buff bricks have been used to good effect in the window arches seen on the right. The S&D became part of the NER in 1863. The station retains its BR(NE) tangerine sign.

Details

Above the cornices of the two end pavilions at Huddersfield station are the coats of arms of the original owning companies: the Lancashire & Yorkshire, and the Huddersfield & Manchester Railway & Canal Company.

Benches often bore the name of the station, as here at Battersby. The lower picture shows a bench on Scarborough Platform 1 which is supposedly the longest station bench in the world.

Top left, at Bingley, on the gable pediment is the MR logo surmounted by a wyvern and surrounded by acanthus leaves. Bottom left, the lion astride the entrance to Glossop station is the symbol of the Howard family. It was the Duke of Norfolk who built the branch from Dinting to Glossop. Top right, at Earlestown, is this extraordinary carving of a man with an oak tree sprouting from his mouth. Bottom right, a different wyvern; this one at Skipton. The MR inherited the wyvern symbol form one of its constituents – the Leicester & Swannington Railway.

Bottom left, a wheeled gate at Arbroath. Top right, another wheeled gate; this one at Hessle, together with a scale for parcels traffic. Top left, the balusters of the footbridge at Cark & Cartmel. Bottom right, a kissing gate at Nairn.

The drinking fountain at Pitlochry, on the left, was originally at Strathyre on the Callander & Oban Railway. The station clock at Perth, built by James Ritchie & Son of Edinburgh, probably in the 1880s, is seen on the right. When this photograph was taken, it was still being hand wound; later, an autowinder was fitted.

Spandrels were often used to display company logos. Top left, the G&SWR logo at Kilmarnock. Top right, FR's crest at Ulverston. The lower left photograph was taken at Hellifield. Bottom right, the NER crest and the white rose of Yorkshire, seen at York.

An NER diagram 60 barrow at Filey.

Abandoned at Morecambe is this MR type 210 barrow.

Delivering the Goods

Goods Warehouses

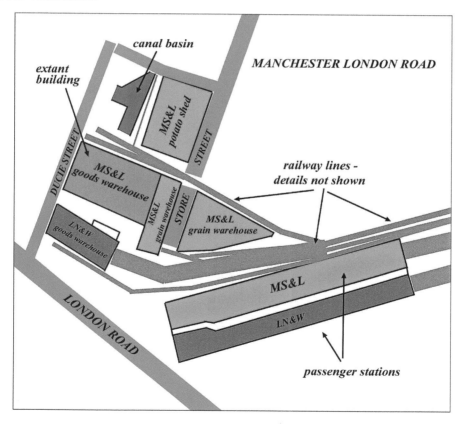

Today's railway is essentially a passenger railway, and so the previous importance of the transport of goods by the railway may be overlooked. This plan makes clear just how important that part of the business was. This was the Manchester London Road station in the late nineteenth century. The two railway companies shared the passenger station but each had their own goods facilities. The space devoted to goods traffic was far greater than that for passengers.

Happily, one of these buildings has survived. It is the main MS&L goods warehouse, dating from 1867. An almost square building, ten bays by nine, and seven storeys high, it is built of brown brick with sandstone quoins, cornice and parapet. Wagons would have been shunted in through the openings, now bricked up, while road vehicles would have entered through the two pairs of doorways on the left-hand side.

Each of the railway companies would have had their own goods facilities in Manchester. The massiveness of the GNR warehouse emphasises once again the vast extent of this traffic. Designed by W. T. Foxlee and dating from 1899, it has five storeys and measures 267 feet by 217 feet. It is built of red and blue brick with stone dressings, and has a dentilled cornice. What is remarkable about this building is that the two lower floors were two separate goods stations; the upper one for London traffic, and the lower one for other destinations.

The Midland Railway depot in Liverpool was constructed in 1872 to the design of Henry Sumners. It is of red brick on a rusticated stone plinth, with stone dressings and bands, and a stone cornice with modillions. The window arches are picked out in contrasting coloured brick. This photograph was taken in 1989. In the mid-1990s the building was converted into a conservation centre for the Liverpool museums. It is now the National Conservation Centre.

The Cheshire Lines Committee goods warehouse at Warrington proudly proclaims the CLC constituent companies. A decorative effect has been achieved by the use of contrasting coloured brick and hexagonal paned windows. The latter was very much a Midland Railway speciality. Wagons would have been shunted in through the openings on the shorter end of the building, while goods would have been loaded to road vehicles from the openings on the longer side. Goods would also have been lowered by crane from the two loopholes above each opening. The warehouse has since become apartments.

The joint LNW/LYR goods warehouse at Huddersfield was completed in 1885. It is constructed from red brick with blue brick strings and dressings, and it has a dentilled cornice. A hydraulically powered hoist supported on massive cast-iron columns raised wagons to the second floor. Goods could also be raised or lowered by cranes into and out of the loopholes (blue-painted doors).

The hydraulic power was provided by this boiler and pump house and accumulator tower. The Italianate tower is thought to be an older building than the boiler house, which is a later replacement. The different styles of architecture would tend to support this.

This is one of the most important early railway buildings. It was the terminus of the Leeds & Selby Railway, which opened in 1834. The building was designed by James Walker and George Smith, and built by Atack & Boothman. The station had six tracks: the two outer pairs were for goods and extended through the two arched openings seen here across the road to jetties on the river bank, while the two middle lines were for passengers. When the line was extended to Hull in 1840 a new station was built and this building became exclusively a goods depot. The central openings were created in 1841 and the former passenger tracks were also extended to jetties on the river bank. The office block on the left was a later NER addition.

Goods Sheds

We come now to a building that virtually every station would have had: the goods shed. The example here at Leeming Bar is a typical design of G. T. Andrews. It is a simple building in brick with entry for wagons in the return and two openings in the long side for the transfer of goods to road vehicles. The goods office completes the picture. This building is listed Grade II, but for some inexplicable reason English Heritage lists this as a locomotive shed.

Nafferton is another building by G. T. Andrews, and was built in 1846 for the York & North Midland Railway. It is similar in overall style to Leeming Bar but with the addition of a stone string course and Diocletian windows. At the far end is a later extension, which consists of weatherboarding supported on cast-iron columns. Two further points to note: the loading platform on the left, and the red and white 'harlequin' sign on the right corner of the return wall. This indicated that there was limited clearance between the wall and the adjacent track.

The goods shed at Stonehaven, on the Arbroath to Aberdeen line, was constructed for the Caledonian Railway towards the end of the nineteenth century. The main goods shed is a lapped-boarded timber-framed structure, while the office is built of brick. It is listed category B.

At Keith we have the reverse situation, with a coursed stone rubble goods shed and a lapped-boarded office. Notice the large stack of timber on the right, waiting to be loaded. This was still an important traffic for rail at this time (1991).

The goods shed at Drigg was in the Furness Railway 'house style'. The buildings could be of random rubble with stone dressings, as here, or of brick, as elsewhere, but the style remained the same. The distinguishing features were the pilasters descending to form buttresses and the large lunettes. Drigg signal box is a *c.* 1874 FR type 1 box. The ground signal is for the Down to Up crossover. The white lozenge indicates that the line is track-circuited.

The goods shed at Blackburn is included due to the fact that it is a very rare example of a goods shed still being used for the movement of goods. On 12 June 1996, No. 56046 draws forward with 6E41, the Backburn–Lackenby steel empties. The much altered goods shed is built of snecked rubble and is the premises of Gilbraith Transtore.

Small Sheds

Now we came to the goods shed for smaller or less busy stations. The shed at Brompton on the Northallerton–Stockton line is built of brick in Scottish bond. A wagon or two can be shunted inside and goods can be retrieved from the opening protected with an awning in the side wall. The chimney indicates that the goods office in this case is inside the actual shed.

Similar in size and shape is Lealhom, on the Middlesbrough–Whitby line, but in this case it is built of square coursed rubble. Once again the location of the chimney indicates an internal office.

Despite its small size, some thought has gone into the design of the goods shed at Sedgefield. It is built in English garden wall bond with panelled walls and a sawtooth course below the eaves. Goods here would have been simply manhandled from the wagons into the building.

Equipment

Certain bulk goods, typically coal, needed to be weighed when leaving the goods yard. Most stations were equipped with a weighbridge, such as the one here at Forres. Next to the weighbridge was the weighbridge hut, inside which was the weighing equipment. When this photograph was taken in 1991 the equipment inside the hut was complete and intact. Notice the construction of the hut – battened boarding with a cast-iron roof, a style much loved by the Highland Railway.

Another piece of equipment found in the goods yard was the loading gauge. When goods were loaded into open wagons it was important to ensure that they were within gauge. This example, slowly being lost in the undergrowth, is at Blair Atholl.

To load and unload such wagons a crane was normally needed. Such cranes were, for the most part, hand operated. This one is in Arbroath yard.

Coal

At one time every station received supplies of coal for domestic use. These would be delivered to the station yard, where the coal merchant often had his business. In 1961 this traffic amounted to 28 million tons per annum. Beeching did not approve of this and in the 1960s a network of coal concentration depots was set up, from where merchants could collect their supplies. Despite this it is clear that in 1980, when this photograph was taken, wagon loads of coal were still being delivered to some stations. This is Crianlarich.

In 1991 Annan yard is still busy with coal and clearly the merchant has his business here, though whether the supplies of coal actually arrived by rail is difficult to say.

One method of delivering coal to stations was by the use of coal drops, as here at Egton Bridge. Wagons would be shunted along the top of the drops and the different grades of coal would be dropped into the bunkers, where they would be accessible to the merchants.

Other Traffic

This is the siding for the Manchester abattoir at Newton Heath. Cattle would have been led from the wagons into the pens and thence to the slaughterhouse. In 1961 BR still had 5,000 cattle wagons, but it was a traffic in decline, and it ceased altogether in 1975.

The railways had depots in the big cities specifically for fruit and vegetable traffic. This one at Edge Hill, Liverpool, was built by the LNW in 1881. This building, constructed from three different coloured bricks with ashlar dressings, shows some thought in its design. Unfortunately, no thought was given to its historical importance, and it was demolished.

A traffic still carried by rail is scrap metal. This is the yard of Crossley Evans at Shipley. The yard has its own Hunslet shunter – No. HE7159 *Prince of Wales*.

Signalling and Signs

Signalling

Perhaps no building is more characteristic of the railway then the signal box. In 1948 British Railways inherited 10,000 working boxes; by 2012 this total had been reduced to 500, and since then many more have closed. It is the plan of Network Rail that eventually all train movements will be controlled from just fourteen signalling centres. Seen here is Hunmanby, on the Hull–Scarborough line. It is a typical NER type S1a box, which has been extended at some point. It was abolished in 2000.

Oxmardyke is another NER S1a box. Features of this design are the small operating room windows, brick construction in English garden wall bond, corner buttresses resting on corbelled brickwork, sandstone sills and string course. Oxmardyke differs from Hunmanby in having stone arches to the locking room windows, rather than brick. The S1 type was a very long-lived design; the first of this type was built in 1873 and the last in 1903. Oxmardyke, now reduced to the status of a gate box, was built in 1901.

Billingham-on-Tees came within the northern division of the NER and this tall box, dating from 1904, is typical in its hipped roof design. It controls the junction of the line to Sunderland and the freight branch to Seal Sands, and has a McKenzie & Holland No. 17 pattern fifty-lever frame. Points of interest include the 1891 pattern cast-iron station footbridge (the station was closed in 1966, to be replaced by a new one further north), the pair of signals on wooden dolls on a steel gantry, and the motorised boom crossing gates. The gantry has now been replaced by a pair of individual signals on steel posts, and the boom gates by lifting barriers.

When this photograph was taken in 1991, the Leamside line was still in use as a double track freight line. Later that same year the line was closed, and some years later the track was lifted. Fencehouses was an unusual signal box, oversailing on both sides due to the Lambton colliery lines passing behind the box. It was opened in 1912, closed in 1991 and subsequently demolished.

Winning box is an NER type N2, the distinguishing feature being the row of three locking room windows with stone sills and lintels. Opened in 1895, it controls the junction of the freight-only lines to Bedlington and Ashington.

The McKenzie & Holland No. 16 fifteen-lever frame in Winning box. The instruments are BR standard types.

The NER constructed a number of these overtrack signal boxes. This example at Hexham was built in 1896. Note that the gantry is supported at one end by a substantial brick wall, and at the other by cast-iron columns. A similar arrangement exists at Wylam, the location of the only other signal box of this type. Hexham signal box is listed Grade II.

It is doubtful whether many people entering York station have any idea that what confronts them is a signal box, or rather was. It was constructed in the early twentieth century and abandoned in 1951 when a new signal box was opened. The eagle-eyed might spot the roof vent, which is typical of northern division signal boxes. The operating room is now a coffee bar.

Poulton No. 3 signal box sits at the junction of the Fleetwood and Blackpool North lines. It was constructed by the L&Y in 1896 to a Railway Signalling Company design and is fitted with an L&Y seventy-four-lever frame. With the completion of the Fylde resignalling in anticipation of electrification, it has become redundant. Network Rail wish to demolish the box and a campaign has been launched by the Poulton & Wyre Railway Society to save it due to its historical importance. When this photograph was taken in 1990 the lines to Fleetwood (those behind the signal box) were still in use. Freight traffic ceased in 1999 and the lines have now been severed at the junction.

Another L&Y box was the 1892-built Blackpool No. 2. Originally named Blackpool Talbot Road 'A', it was given its present name in 1932. It was originally fitted with a 120-lever L&Y frame, which was later reduced to eighty-three. From 2011, following the closure of Blackpool No. 1, it was the only signal box at Blackpool North. It was taken out of use and demolished in November 2017.

Another view of No. 2 looking towards the country. Note that some of the signals are worked electrically, and also the 'stencil box' route indicators. All of this has now gone following the Fylde resignalling.

Parbold is on the L&Y Wigan to Southport line. It is a Saxby & Farmer type 9 box dating from 1877 and is a listed structure. The photograph dates from September 1989 when lifting barriers were being installed.

The unusual, and probably unique, signal box at the north end of Carnforth station was built by the Furness Railway *c.* 1882. It was probably designed to match the Tudor-style rebuilding of Carnforth station by William Tite, which took place at about the same time. At its north end it has the motto of the Cavendish family, '*cavendo tutus*', reflecting the involvement of the Duke of Devonshire in the FR. It has been out of use since 1903.

Morecambe is a very typically Midland Railway signal box, in this case type 4b. Dating from 1907, it had a ninety-seven-lever frame. It was abolished in 1994 and subsequently demolished.

Wennington Junction is a MR type 2a box, opened in 1890. It was renamed Wennington in the mid-1970s although it had ceased to control a junction after 1967, following the closure of the line through Halton to Lancaster, but as can be seen in this 1990 photograph the nameboard was not changed. It spent most of its time switched out after 1988 and was finally removed and donated to the Poulton & Wyre Railway Society in 2006.

Monks Siding box dates from 1875. It still has its original twenty-lever LNW tumbler frame. A type 3, it represents the first LNW design used universally across the system. It was very much a development of earlier Saxby & Farmer boxes. In this view looking west, the signal on the left is the Up home 1 signal, while the motor-worked distant signal acted as an outer distant for both Crosfields Crossing and Litton Mill. The two ground signals on the left were for the sidings beyond the box, which have since been lifted.

The enormous Caledonian signal box at Stirling Middle opened in 1901. It was fitted with a ninety-six-lever frame in BR days. The lattice signal posts and ball and spike finials are typical of Stevens & Sons, a company which did work for many of the Scottish railway companies.

The lower quadrant subsidiary signal routed trains from the platform line to the Up loop. This was the last surviving Caledonian lower quadrant signal in Scotland. It has now been removed to the Bo'ness & Kinneil Railway.

The signal box at Stonehaven is a Caledonian Railway (northern division) type 2 box installed in 1902. It has a forty-lever frame. A feature – as with so many Scottish boxes, but unknown in England – is the central bay window. It is a listed building owing to its rarity. Very few such type 2 boxes now remain.

Longforgan is something of an oddity. Even though the LMS had settled on a standard box design, the Scottish division continued to build boxes to its own design, as here at Longforgan, which opened in 1929. As well as the bay window, it has another uniquely Scottish feature, a sprocketed roof.

The unusual oversailing signal box at Arbroath North is a variation on the North British type 7 design. Dating from 1911, it contains a seventy-two-lever Stevens & Sons frame. An unusual feature is the dogleg staircase supported on a massive brick pillar. The box is a listed structure, and the cast-iron footbridge seen to the left of the signal box is also listed.

Right and below: Broughty Ferry signal box is unusual for a number of reasons. All-timber boxes are quite rare and this one has been extended onto wooden beams to accommodate a longer frame. Perhaps its most unusual features are seen from the other side. The footbridge passes through the base of the signal box, and the signalman, descending to work the gates, also has to pass through the base of his box. The gates themselves are also odd; manually worked gates consist usually of just a single pair, which makes working them easier, rather than four as here. Note the decorative gate posts and the supporting rods, which can be adjusted for gate drop. Broughty Ferry was opened in 1887 and went out of use in 1995. It is a listed structure.

Above and below: Nairn was the last Highland Railway station with signal boxes at each end of the loop. The signalling instruments were in the main station building and the cabins each contained just a lever frame. The signalman was equipped with a bicycle to enable him to cycle from one box to the other. Both boxes date from 1891 and are McKenzie & Holland type 3/Highland. The first photograph shows Nairn East box, and the second shows the West box, with the East box just visible in the distance. The boxes were abolished in 2000 and the line is now controlled from Inverness.

Girvan signal box, a GSWR type 3 dating from 1893, is a rare survivor. Very few other GSWR boxes survive. It was modified in the early twentieth century, including a very obvious two-bay extension.

Barrhill is the last place in the UK where Tyer's tablets are used to control train movements. This pair of Tyer's Electric Tablet No. 6 machines are in the station office. They control the single lines north to Glenwilly and south to Dunragit.

This type of ground signal is similar in function to the more familiar white disc with red band, with one difference, in that it may be passed in the 'on' position for shunting movements along a headshunt. The headshunt in this particular case, which is at Auchterarder, can be seen on the left.

This gantry at Carnforth Furness & Midland Junction illustrates the situation of signals for lines of equal importance or speed. The left-hand signals are for the line to Wennington and the right-hand pair for Carnforth station. It is clear that there was a third pair of signals on the right, which were for a line that bypassed Carnforth station to the west to reach the West Coast Main Line (see map). The signal box and signals have long gone. There is no longer a through route to Wennington and the lines in this area have been completely remodelled.

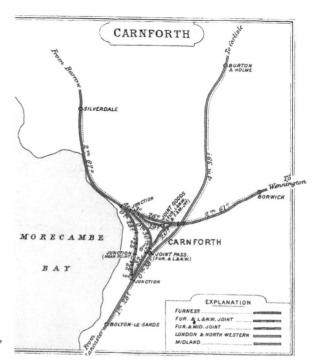

The layout of the lines around Carnforth, as they were before the First World War.

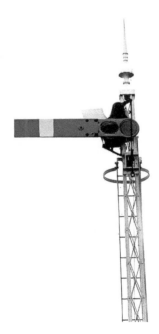

The signal on the left is the Down home at Girvan. The subsidiary signal controls the crossover for entry into the goods yard. On the right is the Dunkeld Down and Up main starter signal with its magnificent McKenzie & Holland 'parachute and spike' finial.

Signals on the Hendon branch can be seen on the left. The signal box and these signals are long gone. On the right, a pair of short arm signals are seen at the end of the Down platform at Barnsley station. The left-hand signal is for the line to Huddersfield, and the right-hand one is for Wakefield. In the background is Barnsley Station Junction signal box, which has since been abolished.

This unusual signal is PP1 62 of Philip's Park No. 1 signal box, which is seen in the background. The colour light signal acted as an outer distant for Miles Platting and Brewery Sidings. The semaphore had its green aspect blanked out, but when it was pulled off the colour light could show single or double yellow or green. The box was abolished in 1998.

Lineside Signs

The railways were compelled by an Act of 1845 to erect markers at quarter-mile intervals along their tracks. This was partly to ensure that passengers had been charged the correct fare, but more importantly to enable trains, especially when failed, to be located, and for engineering and maintenance purposes. Traditionally distances have always been in miles and chains. Each company had its own style of milepost. On the left, an MSL milepost at Philips Park has been supplemented by a BR concrete type. The 'M' is for Manchester. The Midland Railway milepost on the right is on the Grassington branch. The disc reads 'from E Jcn'; E in this case being Embsay.

The NER had a very good system. The mileposts indicated to which location the distance shown related, in this case Hull. The intermediate posts had one to three 'spikes', indicating 1/4, 1/2, or 3/4. An example of a 3/4 post can be seen adjacent to the NER warning sign, which appears below. The Caledonian Railway used different shapes to indicate the intermediate distances: a triangle for 1/4, an oval for 1/2, as here at Auchterarder, and a rectangle for 3/4.

Another important piece of information on the lineside for train crews, especially in steam days, was the gradient post. This example was at Usworth on the now closed Leamside line.

The railway companies were very careful to define the extent of their property. This boundary marker is at Langho on the L&Y's Blackburn–Hellifield line.

Seen at Cave, on the Selby–Hull line, is this warning to potential trespassers. These signs were to be found all over the NER system. Note the NER 3/4 milepost.

Much less common is this Railway Executive sign located at Kennethmont on the Aberdeen–Inverness line. The Railway Executive, which was part of the British Transport Commission, existed only from 1948 to 1953.

Also less common are signs erected by the CLC. This warning about weight restrictions was on a bridge crossing the railway at Sankey.

Station signs

This sign at Honley in West Yorkshire has three things in its favour over more modern signs. It is clear, elegant and durable. It consists of painted cast-iron letters screwed on to a wooden baseboard.

There is no doubt that the signs conceived for the newly nationalised British Railways were the best on any railway. They were clear, durable (being made of enamelled steel), elegant and colourful. Different colours were allocated to each region: green for the Southern, brown for the Western, maroon for the London Midland, dark blue for the Eastern, pale blue for the Scottish Region, and tangerine for the North Eastern. The North Eastern Region lasted only until 1967, after which it became part of the Eastern Region. This is the running-in board at Barnsley station.

As well as the running-in boards, each station would have a series of smaller signs that became known as 'totems'. These were replaced by black and white signs during the 'corporate image' phase of BR. This is a late survivor.

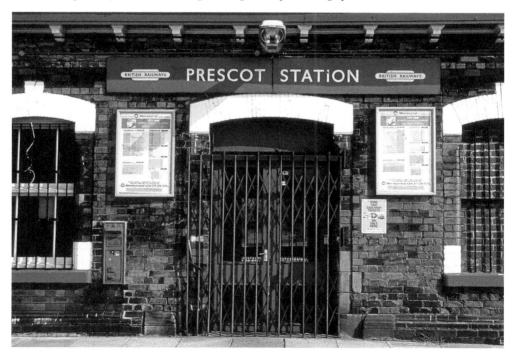

A particularly fine example on the exterior of Prescot station, which survived at least until 1992, when this photograph was taken. It was later replaced by a standard black and white sign.

Other Structures

Carriage Sheds

In the days of steam the almost universal concept of a train was of an engine and carriages. The railways of Britain had an enormous number of carriages; in 1962, British Railways still possessed more than 22,000. Accordingly, a large number of carriage sheds were needed to maintain, clean and store these vehicles. The shrinking of the railway following the Beeching cuts and the change from hauled coaches to fixed formations of various kinds led to most carriage sheds becoming redundant, as here at Stourton, near Leeds. In a somewhat dilapidated condition, Stourton carriage shed is seen on 27 August 1989.

It wasn't entirely the end of such structures, although a new kind of building was required for more modern vehicles, as here at Longsight, near Manchester. This depot was built in the early 1990s in anticipation of the start of regional Eurostars. Following the decision not to continue with the regional trains, the depot stood empty for ten years. Since that time it has had periods of usage, including by Siemens for their new Class 185 DMUs. The panel on the side reads '*le eurostar habite ici*'. If only...

Engine Sheds and Servicing

Redundant, too, were the many steam locomotive sheds. Some were converted to house diesels but the majority were either demolished or sold off. Blair Atholl is a two-road shed in squared coursed rubble with a corrugated iron roof. At some point the roof was heightened by the addition of two courses of brick, and additional ventilation was provided. It was a sub-shed of Perth and closed in 1966.

The Caledonian engine shed at Stranraer has also undergone roof heightening by the insertion of additional brick courses. Otherwise, it was built of snecked rubble with ashlar dressings. With the shed code 67F, it closed in 1966.

One of the disadvantages of the steam locomotive was its need to be turned in order to return from where it came. Consequently, there was a very large number of turntables, particularly at terminal stations. A few survive today, including this example at Scarborough, which gets extensive use turning the locomotives off steam specials.

Other needs of the steam engine were coal and water. Most stations would have had water columns at the end of their platforms. A number of these water columns survive, as here at Skipton. It is complete apart from the loss of the leather 'bag'. It bears the wording 'MR Co.' It would originally have had a top-mounted lamp.

This water column, seen at Wigton in 1995, was still complete with its leather 'bag'. 'Putting the bag in' was enginemen's talk for filling the tender with water.

During the winter months, braziers were often located next to water columns to prevent freezing. The NER had a more ingenious idea; they actually put a fire inside the column, which had a double skin. The fire door hole and smoke vents can be clearly seen on this example at Haltwhistle. This, and another at the same location, are listed structures.

Also listed is the tank and supporting structure that supplied the columns. The building is of sandstone ashlar and the tank is cast iron. The plate reads 'PETER TATE ENGINEER 1861 R. WYLIE & Co. NEWCASTLE TYNE'.

A less common type of water column was this 'parachute' water column, which had its own reservoir. This example was at Skipton. It has now been removed to the Embsay & Bolton Abbey Steam Railway.

Yet another historically significant structure is this brick building and tank at Knaresborough, constructed for the York & North Midand Railway in 1851. The cast iron-tank was probably built by James Walker of Leeds. Both the building, which was originally the lamp room, and the tank are listed Grade II.

At Seascale on the Cumbrian Coast line is this extraordinary, and possibly unique, water tower, which was built for the Furness Railway. It is built of rock-faced red sandstone with ashlar bands and dressings, surmounted by a conical slate roof with a finial. It's interesting to speculate about the purpose of the chimney. Close by is the former goods shed, constructed in typical FR style.

Two important structures from the steam age are the coaling plant and ash plant at Carnforth depot. They were commissioned by the LMS in 1938 and were in use by 1940. They are rare survivors and their importance is reflected by their being listed Grade II.

This is a picture of another coaling facility, but which was taken by accident! The photographer was mainly interested in the loading gauge and only realised later that the ramp on the left was an important historical structure – the coaling ramp at Shildon. Wagons of coal were pushed up the incline; locomotives then came alongside and coal was loaded into the tenders via chutes. These coal drops date from *c.* 1856 and are listed Grade II.

Bridges, Viaducts and Tunnels

The railway age produced some impressive engineering, probably the most spectacular of which were the viaducts. Penistone Viaduct was completed in 1849 for the Huddersfield & Sheffield Junction Railway. Consisting of twenty-nine arches and 330 yards long, it was designed by Sir John Hawkshaw and built by the contractors Ingham & Bower. The eagle-eyed will notice that the DMU crossing the viaduct in 1980 is a hybrid. The two left-hand vehicles are Class 110, while the third vehicle is a Class 101.

Possibly the most famous viaduct in Britain is the Ribblehead or Batty Moss Viaduct. Designed by John Crossley, it was built for the Midland Railway between 1870 and 1874. It is 440 yards long, 104 feet high and consists of twenty-four spans. More than 100 navvies died during its construction. In the winter of 1988, No. 47588 heads north across the viaduct with a diverted WCML service.

North Seaton Viaduct spans the River Wansbeck on the freight-only Blyth & Tyne line. It was built in 1927 by the Cleveland Bridge Company to replace an earlier wooden structure. It has fourteen spans and is 1,024 feet long, and one of only two surviving all-metal viaducts are still in use.

Enterkine Viaduct is a wrought-iron, plate-girder bridge supported on stone piers. It was constructed in 1872 to carry the Killoch–Annbank freight branch across the River Ayr. On 1 August 1995 a pair of Class 37s cross the viaduct with a train of coal for Killoch Washery.

Arnside or Kent Viaduct, on the Cumbrian Coast line, was built in 1856 to carry the Ulverston & Lancaster Railway across the estuary of the River Kent. It consisted of a lattice girder superstructure supported on fifty brick piers, giving a total length of 550 yards. In 2010/11 the superstructure was completely replaced. On 6 June 1992, Stanier 8F No. 48151 crosses the viaduct with a Barrow–Carnforth shuttle.

To cross navigable waterways, the railway often employed swing bridges, as here at Selby on the line to Hull. This asymmetric, wrought-iron bridge was designed by Thomas Harrison of the NER and was put in place in 1891, replacing an earlier structure. Hydraulic power to move the bridge was originally provided by a pair of accumulators housed in the brick tower seen on the right. This was later superseded by an electro-hydraulic system.

Network Rail is said to be responsible for 40,000 bridges, tunnels and viaducts. The vast majority of these will be fairly simple structures, such as this stone bridge on the trans-Pennine main line. It employs voussoirs in the arch. These are five-sided blocks that allow the squared blocks in the spandrels to butt up neatly to the arch. The Class 47 is hauling a Newcastle–Liverpool service near Marsden in 1981.

Another type of bridge seen at almost every station is the footbridge. Here at Kirkby Stephen the stonework around the supports and stairways shows that this cast-iron bridge has, at some time, been raised. This may have been the result of deep ballasting raising the rail height. The bridge is a listed structure.

Cast iron was a commonly used material for footbridges. Much less frequently found was wood, as here at Hassendean on the closed Waverley route.

The first Standedge tunnel was completed in 1848, to be followed by a second in 1871. These are the two tunnels on the right, mostly obscured by vegetation. The double-track tunnel on the left was opened in 1898; it is 3 miles 66 yards long and is the only tunnel of the three still in use (the 1848 and 1871 tunnels closed in 1966 and 1970 respectively). Believe it or not, this view shows Diggle station. One of the platform edges can just be seen. Standedge tunnel contained the only piece of level track on the whole trans-Pennine route and thus it was here that the water troughs were installed. The tank that supplied them can be seen on the platform.

Other Buildings

Today's railway traveller may sometimes see small huts by the lineside. These were the platelayers' cabins, where the men who worked on the permanent way could take their breaks. This first is a nice stone-built example on the Highland Railway at Keith.

Somewhat less attractive, but sturdy enough, is a brick-built cabin at Barrhill.

Many cabins were simple wooden structures. Still wearing its LMR colours is this cabin constructed of battened boarding, seen at Hellifield in 1989.

The railway companies built houses for their employees, not least to ensure that they would always be on hand. This accommodation was usually built to a high standard, as here at Kirkby Stephen. There are six railway workers' cottages, with the stationmaster's house on the right, somewhat obscured by trees.

To accommodate travellers, most major stations had an adjoining hotel, which was built and owned by the railway company. This is the NER-built Royal Station Hotel at York, dating from 1878 and designed by the architect William Peachey. It is built of yellow Scarborough brick with ashlar quoins, bands and dressings. It was sold off by British Railways in 1983 and is now known as the Principal Hotel.

In 1920 the NER commissioned Sir Edwin Lutyens, who was renowned for this kind of work, to design a war memorial to commemorate the 2,236 men of the company who died in the First World War. It was also Lutyens who designed the cenotaph in Whitehall. The memorial, built of limestone, was unveiled in June 1924 and has the names of all those who died inscribed on its walls. It is located just inside the city walls of York and is listed Grade II.